POEMS FROM GUANTÁNAMO

POEMS FROM

Guan

UNIVERSITY OF IOWA PRESS   Iowa City

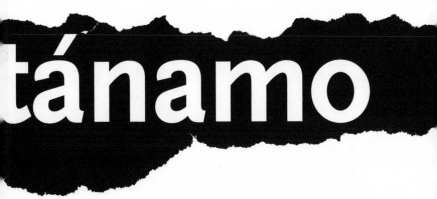

THE DETAINEES SPEAK

Edited by MARC FALKOFF

Preface by FLAGG MILLER

Afterword by ARIEL DORFMAN

University of Iowa Press, Iowa City 52242

Copyright © 2007 by the University of Iowa Press

Afterword copyright © 2007 by Ariel Dorfman

www.uiowapress.org

Printed in the United States of America

Design by Richard Hendel

The University of Iowa Press is a member of Green Press Initiative and
is committed to preserving natural resources.

Printed on acid-free paper

Library of Congress Cataloging-in-Publication Data
Poems from Guantánamo: the detainees speak / edited by Marc Falkoff;
preface by Flagg Miller; afterword by Ariel Dorfman.
p.   cm.
Includes bibliographical references.
ISBN-13: 978-1-58729-606-2 — ISBN-10: 1-58729-606-3
1. Prisoners' writings, Arabic — Cuba — Guantánamo Bay Naval Base —
Translations into English.   2. Prisoners' writings, Pushto — Cuba —
Guantánamo Bay Naval Base — Translations into English.   3. Arabic
poetry — Translations into English.   4. Pushto poetry — Translations
into English.   5. Guantánamo Bay Naval Base (Cuba) — Poetry.   6. War
on Terrorism, 2001– — Poetry.   I. Falkoff, Marc.
PJ7694.E3P56   2007
892.7'170809729167 — dc22   2007007345

For my friends inside the wire,

Mahmoad, Majid, Yasein, Saeed,

Abdulsalam, Mohammed, Adnan,

Jamal, Othman, Adil, Mohamed,

Abdulmalik, Aref, Sadeq, Farouk,

Salman, and Makhtar.

Inshallah, we will next meet over

coffee in your homes in Yemen.

M. F.

CONTENTS

ACKNOWLEDGMENTS

This collection would not exist if not for the efforts of the hundreds of volunteer lawyers, professors, paralegals, law students, and human rights advocates who have worked tirelessly to restore the rule of law to Guantánamo Bay. Before the lawyers began to open it up, Guantánamo was truly a "black hole" from which no information—and certainly not the voices of the detainees—could escape.

In this regard, the leadership of the Center for Constitutional Rights has been particularly important. Long before major law firms joined the fold, CCR lawyers were spearheading efforts to mount *habeas corpus* challenges on behalf of the detainees. For more than five years, past and present CCR lawyers—including J. Wells Dixon, Tina Monshipour Foster, Bill Goodman, Gitanjali Gutierrez, Emi MacLean, Joseph Margulies, Barbara Olshansky, and Michael Ratner—have been instrumental in organizing the legal community's response to Guantánamo.

Collecting the poems in this volume required the assistance of many overworked *habeas* lawyers and was no easy task. Special thanks to my former colleagues at Covington & Burling—David Remes, Trisha Anderson, Eric Carlson, Jason Knott, Robert Knowles, Gregory Lipper, and Brent Starks—as well as to Pat Bronte, Louise Christian, Joshua Colangelo-Bryan, Douglas Cox, Buz Eisenberg, Neha Gohil, Sarah Havens, Zachary Katznelson, Neil McGaraghan, Susan Baker Manning, Brent Mickum, Gareth Peirce, Anant Raut, Sylvia Royce, Amanda Shafer, Clive Stafford Smith, Scott Sullivan, Ian Wallach, Sabin Willet, and Elizabeth Wilson. Thanks also to the law students and legal assistants who have helped with the project, including Seema Ahmad, Jessica Baen, Alysha Beckwith, Elizabeth Braverman, Nicole Hillman, Susan Hu, Omolara Johnson, Alissa King, Christopher Lynch, Dan McLean, and Greg Welikson.

Finally, a word of appreciation to the translators, who were frequently working under extraordinary conditions both at Guantánamo and in a "secure facility" in Virginia, where our clients' letters and other classified materials are stored. They provided us with translations of our clients' writings, often under tight deadlines and without access to the usual dictionaries and other tools of the trade. Among them are Marwan Abdel-Rahman, Felice Bezri, Luna Droubi, Abu Jalal, Mahmoud Khatib, Flagg Miller, Khalid al Odah, Clive Stafford Smith, and Fuad Yahya.

POEMS FROM GUANTÁNAMO

NOTES ON GUANTÁNAMO

MARC FALKOFF

The twenty-two poems in this volume were written by men held in the United States military detention center in Guantánamo Bay, Cuba. Like all the prisoners in Guantánamo, the poets are Muslim. A number have been released to their home countries, but most are enduring their sixth year of captivity in near-total isolation, imprisoned without charge, trial, or the most fundamental protections of the Geneva Conventions. Their poems, all written "inside the wire," were composed with little expectation of ever reaching an audience beyond a small circle of their fellow prisoners. But now that the poems have been declassified and collected, they offer the world a unique opportunity to hear directly from the detainees themselves about their time in America's notorious prison camp.

My colleagues and I—all volunteer lawyers—first visited Guantánamo in November 2004, after receiving "secret" level security clearances from the FBI. What we learned from our clients on that trip was shocking. During the three years in which they had been held in total isolation, they had been repeatedly abused. They had been subjected to stress positions, sleep deprivation, blaring music, and extremes of heat and cold during endless interrogations. They had been sexually humiliated, their physical space invaded by female interrogators who taunted them, fully aware of the insult they were meting out to devout Muslims. They were denied basic medical care. They were broken down and psychologically tyrannized, kept in extreme isolation, threatened with rendition, interrogated at gunpoint, and told that their families would be harmed if they refused to talk. They were also frequently prevented from engaging in their daily prayers (one of the five pillars of Islam) and forced to witness American soldiers intentionally mishandling the holy Qur'an.

At first, there was little we could do with this information. Anything our clients told us, the military explained, represented a potential national security threat and therefore could not be revealed to the public until cleared by a Pentagon "Privilege Review Team." The review team, in turn, initially used its power to suppress all evidence of abuse and mistreatment. Our notes, returned with a "classified" stamp, were deemed unsuitable for public release on the grounds that they revealed interrogation techniques that the military had a legitimate interest in keeping secret. Only when threats of litigation forced the Pentagon to reconsider its classification decisions did the public finally begin to hear, albeit in a mediated way, from the detainees themselves.

This volume represents another step in our struggle to allow our clients' voices to be heard. In truth, it is something of a miracle that the collection — or the poetry that comprises it — even exists. The psychic toll that Guantánamo has taken on the detainees is unfathomable. They remain entirely isolated from the rest of the world, kept ignorant of all current events. All references to contemporary world events are excised from the occasional letters they are allowed to receive from family members, and their lawyers may not tell them any personal or general news unless it directly relates — an arbitrary standard, to be sure — to their cases. It is difficult to see how hope can flourish in such an environment, where the only contact with the outside world is an occasional visit from a lawyer or an infrequent and heavily censored letter from a relative. Indeed, dozens of prisoners have attempted suicide by hanging, by hoarding and then overdosing on medicine, or by slashing their wrists. (The military, in truly Orwellian fashion, has described these suicide attempts as incidents of "manipulative self-injurious behavior." When three detainees successfully killed themselves in June 2006, the military called the suicides acts of "asymmetric warfare.")[1]

Many men at Guantánamo turned to writing poetry as a way to maintain their sanity, to memorialize their suffering, and to preserve their humanity through acts of creation. Confined indefinitely without any meaningful judicial oversight, they follow in the footsteps of prisoners who wrote in the Gulag, the Nazi concentration camps, and, closer to home, the Japanese American internment camps.

The obstacles they have faced in composing their poems are profound. In the first year of their detention, many of the detainees were not allowed regular use of pen and paper. Undeterred, some would draft short poems on Styrofoam cups they had retrieved from their lunch and dinner trays. Lacking writing instruments, they would inscribe their words with pebbles or trace out letters with small dabs of toothpaste, then pass the "cup poems" from cell to cell. The cups would inevitably be collected with the day's trash, the poetic inscriptions consigned to the bottom of a rubbish bin. Two of these poems—by Shaikh Abdurraheem Muslim Dost, a Pakistani poet who was released from Guantánamo in April 2005—were reconstructed from memory and are included in this collection.

After about a year, the military granted the detainees access to regular writing materials, and for the first time they could preserve their poems beyond the end of a meal. The first poem I saw was sent to me by Abdulsalam Ali Abdulrahman Al-Hela, who had written his verses in Arabic after spending extended periods in an isolation cell. The poem is a moving cry about the injustice of arbitrary detention and a hymn to the comforts of religious faith. Soon after I read it, I learned that Adnan Farhan Abdul Latif—another of our clients who has been mercilessly abused while in Guantánamo—had composed a poem of his own called "The Shout of Death." (I cannot comment more on these poems, because the Pentagon has refused to clear them for public inspection.) After querying other lawyers, I learned that Guantánamo was filled with amateur poets.

Many of the poems I have seen address aspects of the men's detention experiences, laying bare their anger at the pain and humiliation they have suffered at the hands of the United States military. Other poems reveal a sense of betrayal and disbelief that Americans—the "protectors of peace," in the words of poet Jumah al Dossari—would deny the detainees even the semblance of justice. But all the poems attest to the humanity of these men, who have been vilified by our government as "the worst of the worst" evildoers on the planet. The administration's sloganeering has effectively disguised the fact that, according to the military's own documents, only eight percent of the detainees are even accused of being al Qaeda fighters, only five percent were captured by United States forces on the battlefields of Afghanistan, and fewer than half are accused of committing a hostile act against the United States.[2]

As a consequence of the restrictive context in which this volume was assembled, the collection inevitably suffers from some flaws. It is not a complete portrait of the poetry composed at Guantánamo, largely because many of the detainees' poems were destroyed or confiscated before they could be shared with the authors' lawyers. The military, for instance, confiscated nearly all twenty-five thousand lines of poetry composed by Shaikh Abdurraheem Muslim Dost, returning to him only a handful upon his release from Guantánamo. "Why did they give me a pen and paper if they were planning to do that?" Dost asked a reporter after his release. "Each word was like a child to me—irreplaceable."

In addition, the Pentagon refuses to allow most of the detainees' poems to be made public, arguing that poetry "presents a special risk" to national security because of its "content and format." The fear appears to be that the detainees will try to smuggle coded messages out of the prison camp. Hundreds of poems therefore remain suppressed by the military and will likely never be seen by the public. In addition, most of the poems that *have* been cleared are in English translation only, because the Pentagon believes that their original Arabic or Pashto versions represent an enhanced security risk. Because only linguists with secret-level security clearances are allowed to read our clients' communications (which are kept by court order in a secure facility in the Washington, D.C., area) it was impossible to invite experts to translate the poems for us. The translations that we have included here, therefore, cannot do justice to the subtlety and cadence of the originals.

Despite these and many other hurdles, this book has now been published. Representative voices of the detainees may now be heard by more than the lawyers who are fighting on their behalf. As the courts move sluggishly toward granting the detainees fair and open hearings, and as politicians bicker about whether to extend Geneva Conventions protections to the detainees, the detainees' own words may now become part of the dialogue. Perhaps their poems will prick the conscience of a nation.

NOTES

1. There have been dozens of press accounts documenting suicide attempts such as these. See, for example, "Detainees Attempted to Hang Selves," *Boston Globe*, January 25, 2005, which cites military documents released through the Freedom of Information Act. After thirty-two such attempts, the military began to reclassify them in September 2003.

2. See Mark Denbeaux and Joshua W. Denbeaux, "Report on Guantánamo Detainees: A Profile of 517 Detainees through Analysis of Department of Defense Data," Seton Hall Public Law Research Paper no. 46, www.cfr.org/publications/9838, accessed February 14, 2007.

FORMS OF SUFFERING IN
MUSLIM PRISON POETRY

FLAGG MILLER

Poetry is born of suffering, as an old Arabic saying goes. Arabic poetry—or shi`r—is also held to be a vessel of insight and perception, one whose rhythms are attuned less to measured thoughts than to wellsprings of raw human feeling, shu`uur. In "Ode to the Sea," Ibrahim al Rubaish draws upon a traditional image of poetry as the sea itself to create verses that both provide relief and stir the depths of bitter despair: "Your stillness will kill the captain if it persists, / And the navigator will drown in your waves. // Gentle, deaf, mute, ignoring, angrily storming, / You carry graves." Poetry from Guantánamo Bay carries a message to humankind that is bittersweet at best. Complacency is not of poetic temperament.

From the earliest days of Islam's rise among world religions in the seventh century, poetry has provided a steady moral compass for Muslims. Its power to inspire believers as well as its controversial use for mischief were both appreciated by the prophet Muhammad. While warning listeners away from the tendency of poets to "aimlessly rove in every valley, preaching what they never practice" (Qur'an 26:225), the Prophet had the good judgment to enlist the support of some of the strongest poets in Arabia. In the centuries that followed, as Islam expanded among diverse communities that knew neither Arabic nor the customs of the Prophet's followers, poets continued to provide eloquent and easily memorized glosses on Islam's core messages. Whether composing in classical Arabic designed for the learned or in regional dialects designed to attract broader and often illiterate audiences, poets were important allies to political leaders.

Poets could also be formidable adversaries. As early Muslim states developed, so too did new means of incarceration, along with the categories of criminal behavior used to justify imprisonment. In the provinces of Kufa, Damascus, Mosul, and coastal Yemen, ill-favored poets were among the first occupants of these early prisons. With emerging notions of civilizational order, responsibility, and social entitlement, however, the prison experience would speak to wider circles of versifiers, including those who, although not literally imprisoned, turned to certain types of verse in order to express the intensity of felt oppression. In genres called *habsiyya*, which emerged during periods of state centralization in Iran after the ninth century, as well as in Pakistan and India, for example, poets drew upon long-established traditions of Persian love poetry to reflect on their own sufferings, on the consolations of writing verse, and the possibilities of spiritual release. Such poetry continued to be refined in later centuries across South Asia and in the Middle East.

At another level, nationalist movements supplied new tools for discussing oppression and the rights of indigenous peoples. Poetry was instrumental, especially rhymed couplets composed in the tradition of Arabic *qasida* verse. Since the Prophet's day, the *qasida*'s formal meters, adjustable length (typically from twelve to eighty verses), and themes both spiritual and quotidian had helped popularize the genre among Muslim communities across Southeast Asia, India, Central Asia, the coasts of Africa, and Europe. *Habsiyya* poets were especially fond of the *qasida*'s structured conventions. As twentieth-century nationalists across the Arab world began enjoying the fruits of liberation struggles against Europe's colonial territories, *qasida* poetry was reworked to express a common cultural heritage. Neoclassical themes such as nostalgia for youthful lovers, descriptions of desert journeys, and praise for patrons found receptive audiences among socialist reformers partly because, although best expressed in Arabic, they also accommodated regional dialects and customs. Moreover, while expressive of

Islamic cultural ideals, they were not exclusively the heritage of Muslims. In diverse political contexts, poets addressed a variety of peoples, nations, and world revolutions.

The challenge for activists was, of course, to keep the *qasida* genre from being co-opted by entrenched national elites and to preserve its flexibility as a weapon for populist dissent. Marxists promoted the use of vernacular, rather than classical, Arabic in efforts to sever the *qasida*'s association with traditions of belles lettres. They also privileged shorter, easier compositions that could be sung as anthems and performed in mass gatherings to stirring musical accompaniment. Palestinians gained renown for their *qasida* anthems, many of which furthered the themes of an emerging prison literature that included short stories and novels by both men and women. With roughly thirty percent of Palestinians in the West Bank and Gaza Strip having passed through Israeli prisons by the 1980s, images of the "cage," the "bird," and, later, the "hurled stone" grew especially popular throughout the Middle East. Socialists in Egypt, South Yemen, Libya, and Morocco, as well as secular Ba`thists in Syria and Iraq, found ample recourse to such images, while Islamists responded to the *qasida*'s potential elitism in multiple ways. Conservative reformers sometimes criticized the practice of poetry altogether, especially if sung or set to musical instrumentation, arguing that Muslims were better served by studying the Qur'an, memorizing transmitted accounts of the Prophet's words and deeds, and pursuing degrees in Islamic law—or *shari`a*—even from the confines of one's prison cell. Other Islamists appreciated the value of poetry in refining one's ethical and political sentiments. As noted by one of the Guantánamo poets, Abdulla Majid al Noaimi, "I set out to write, but I could not concentrate on the poem. I put poetry writing aside and turned to memorizing the Qur'an. But then I could not concentrate on the Qur'an, because my mind was occupied with the poem. With my mind divided, time began to pass. And then I was inspired."

Late twentieth- and twenty-first-century militants could find inspiration for composing poetry in the writings of Egyptian Islamist Sayyid Qutb, considered by many to be the most influential modern theorist of global Islamic resurgence. During the 1950s and 1960s, Qutb was arrested and tortured in the jails of Gamal ʿAbd al-Nasser, the president of Egypt and champion of the Pan-Arab movement. Few institutions in the Arab world would prove as instrumental in turning moderate Islamist reformers, many of them members of Egypt's Muslim Brotherhood, into committed militants. From their ranks rose Anwar Sadat's assassins, whose designation of the Egyptian president as a tyrannical "pharaoh" with close links to the United States (and its White House, or "Palace") is echoed by one of the Guantánamo poets, Ustad Badruzzaman Badr. Many of al-Qaʿida's core leaders were Egyptians who had grown up in the shadow of Nasser's jails (including Ayman al Zawahiri, Abu Hafs, Sayf al ʿAdl, Nasser Fahmi, and others). These men understood well how torture could turn conservative moral reformers into radical militants, so they drew particular attention to ways in which abject humiliation drives victims of torture to seek revenge.[1] Before Qutb had developed his ideas about global *jihad* in the interests of "freedom from servitude," however, his earliest years were spent as a journalist, poet, and literary critic. The poet, Qutb wrote, is no mere philosopher, but is rather an activist who "plunges into life, sensing its sensations, conscious of its consciousness, interacting with it and then speaking about what he senses from it, or else about what life wants to say about itself!"[2] Contrary to the views of many Islamist intellectuals, Qutb held vernacular Arabic to be an especially apt medium for political expression. His interest in wresting poetry from the purview of classically trained aesthetes continues to reflect the orientation of many Islamist populists. Among contributors to this volume, Saudi-born poets (especially Mohammed el Gharani and Abdulla Majid al Noaimi) demonstrate a special interest in the uses of vernacular Arabic for dissent.

Linking broader trends in Muslim prison poetry to the contributions in *Poems from Guantánamo* begs the question of the nature of the Guantánamo poets' dissent. Do the detainees call upon the vocabulary of radical Islamic militancy to defend themselves? Do they invoke other discussions of social justice? To what extent do their verses confirm their designations as global Islamic *jihadists* and "unlawful enemy combatants," as the U.S. administration and military tribunals have maintained?

Part of the challenge of answering such questions lies in the role of poetry as a figurative enterprise. If our aim is to study verbal artistry in a way that is maximally useful, we need to be prepared to consider answers not about the poets' intentions but about our own intentions as analysts responsible for distinguishing fact from fiction. We need to assess not only the detainees' own tendencies toward radicalism but also our own assumptions about detainees' identities, goals, and motivations.

To begin with the nature of poetic dissent in general, it is useful to draw a comparison between the detainees' verse and that of self-proclaimed militant *jihadists*. In this regard, the work of the Guantánamo poets is distinct for its relative absence of overt religious imagery. Militants such as Osama bin Laden himself, renowned among followers for his verse, tend to construct poems around well-rehearsed narratives of Islamic history, especially those focusing on the early armed struggles of Muhammad and his companions. In efforts to highlight their observance of Muslim doctrine, they employ classical Arabic inflected with archaic terms and pronunciations. Seeking a transnational Islamic audience, they avoid marked vernacular diction and themes that once appealed to the nationalist sentiments of Sayyid Qutb and his associates in the Muslim Brotherhood. Poets among the Afghan Arabs are even known to favor compositions bereft of rhyme and meter, in their attempts to shed ties to the nationalist and literary heritage of *qasida* poetry. In such cases, overtly political Islamic symbols become the most important anchor for linking such verse to an envisioned Muslim community.

Barely half the Guantánamo poems in this collection, by contrast, invoke hallmark Islamic terms, such as "Allah," the "book of God," the "messenger," and "Islam." When they are used, moreover, such terms are usually employed in a mainstream manner, inserted into conventional supplications at the end of *qasidas*, rather than being used to develop themes of militancy. Certainly few of these poems open with pious supplications, in contrast to most religious poetry. At first stroke, the Guantánamo poets catch us off guard with a modernism that even rings secular at times. To be sure, studies of Islamic reform movements suggest that many global *jihadists* have a weak understanding of core Muslim beliefs and indeed have more affinity with Marxist revolutionaries than with religious devotees. Rarely do the *jihadists* themselves, however, invite such associations.

If any common theme unites the poems, it is a general concern with physical incarceration and oppression rather than with Islam. Descriptions of imprisonment (*habs*), cages, shackles, and tears provide a shared vocabulary, even as the poets' responses elicit a wide range of emotions. While at times courageous and defiant, the poets at other times express utter defeat, lamentation, and nostalgia, as well as a desire to give good advice. Perhaps most surprising of all, many of the poets share a deep strain of romantic longing. Whether lingering upon images of loved ones or on the flowery pastures of youth, Guantánamo poets have written modern Arabic love poetry. Especially salient are the *qasidas* by Saudi, Bahraini, and Yemeni poets, whose "yearning to meet the loved ones," "tenderest hearts," and gestures of the "kiss on his forehead" evoke trans-Islamic themes of *habsiyya* verse while also deferring to more proximate sentiments expressed in vernacular Arabic.

For those familiar with Arabic poetry, such verses bear an extraordinary resemblance to the florid writings of twentieth-century secular nationalists. Themes of nature's bounty, transcendence, and swimming "salmon" (certainly not found in Arab waters) evoke the work of early nationalist literati who came of age under European colonial rule and were inspired as much by poets like John Keats, William Wordsworth, or Stéphane Mallarmé as they were by neoclassical Arabic traditions. The Guantánamo poets appear to draw even more heavily from the socialist legacies of postcolonial firebrands across the Islamic world. Such influences are found in both themes of forced servitude and the struggle for justice and in the poetic conventions of political anthems such as repetitive anaphora ("We are heroes of the time. / We are the proud youth. / We are the hairy lions.") and open-vowel rhyme schemes that could be easily memorized and sung collectively. A common recourse to simple poetic meters underscores a special engagement with the kind of rural and tribal song traditions that could be picked up by broad audiences. Once again, even if adaptable to performance as Islamic anthems, an extremely popular genre among Muslim reformers worldwide, these poems typically defer overt association with Islamist iconography, as their authors strive to reach a more ecumenical audience.

In trying to come to terms with the oddly contemporary tenor of the poets' contributions, especially their national and socialist sensibilities, we have several possible explanations. From one perspective, we might conclude that the poems are evidence of the detainees' savvy public relations skills and so do not represent their true views as diehard *jihadists* or terrorists. From another, we might point out that the authors may be a self-selected group and that the true radicals are likely keeping quiet. These suggestions, though, are problematic for at least two reasons. Through the ostensible logic of common sense, such positions replace empirical findings, however oblique or confusing, with a far more scripted set of debates about what Muslims or Islamists really want or believe. Rather than acknowledging human experience as complex and, indeed, historically conditioned, they invoke a set of Western stereotypes about the entrenched goals and identities of an "alien enemy." Such assertions are especially disturbing given that almost all the Guantánamo detainees have yet to see their day in court, with even their identities actively mediated by a U.S. administration that struggles to defend a mixed record in its War on Terror.[3]

These arguments also deny the Guantánamo poets' own testimonies of the censorship that hampers their ability to express their responses to the events within the camp. At times, the silence is imposed by prison authorities whose meticulous surveillance of all communications to or from inmates, including postcards from home, is described by one of the contributors in the margins of his poem. Having tried to deliver a photograph of himself to his family through an intermediary, the poet relates his sadness at being told, sometime later, that the intermediary had been forced to swallow the picture just before a complete body search was conducted. More frequently, the source of detainees' censorship is their own self-monitoring. Poetry itself is constraining, a theme that some of the poets explore as they confront the limits of structured verse in their attempts to describe the depths of their suffering. Al Rubaish compares poetry to the sea, whose "beaches are sadness, captivity, pain," and al Noaimi's self-reference as "the Captive of Dignity" expresses his own comparison of sadness to a captive and the embellishments of his dignified verse to the captor. Still, poetry can provide a welcome salve even when its formal devices prove insufficient to express the reality of a tragic situation. In a 2005 study of human rights in Morocco, Susan Slyomovics reports how Moroccan victims of torture hold poetry to be a deeply valued medium because it can communicate that which is too humiliating to acknowledge publicly, especially to relatives at home.[4] Special note might be taken of the stark testimonial poem by Mohammed el Gharani, or the sulfurous verses of Shaikh Abdurraheem Muslim Dost, who writes that one "cannot help but be under the power of the traitors and the notorious. // Consider what might compel a man / to kill himself, or another." Far from being insincere, the Guantánamo poets admit that they have many concealed emotions.

Allowing for the complexity of the detainees' poems is an important first step in restoring a human dimension to grander official narratives about Guantánamo. Alert to the many investments at stake in representing and controlling their identities, the poets struggle intelligently, with what resources they have, to engage the sympathy and responses of the broadest possible audience. Pinioned impossibly in the context of a global war on terror, they seem to realize that a vocabulary of Islamic militancy is poor currency for such ends, even if it were available to given detainees. Instead, the poets strive for a language that is more likely to win advantage: the discourse of universal human rights. This is the claret most likely to linger in the chambers of the world's justice systems, especially those in Western countries. Indeed, as Slyomovics has argued, human rights discourses are entering the repertoires of a growing number of transnational Islamist organizations, especially when their members are incarcerated.[5] At Guantánamo, detainees are preparing their arguments not in sophisticated legal terminology, which most of them lack knowledge of, but rather in the familiar idioms and vocabulary of their youth. Whether describing scenes of nurturing parents or destitute children, of valiant siblings bound by fate or worldwide victory for the oppressed, the idioms most apt for the detainees are those drawn from populist discourses of Arab national liberation.

If the poems surprise us by their return to a political vocabulary of the past, they also remind us of the enduring power in crosscultural responses to global inequality. The ultimate reception of the detainees' verse is likely to be as varied as the aims of the poets, rendered in as many strains as an anthem can have. However construed, the poets strike a deep chord with many audiences, reminding them of the stunted nature of justice at Guantánamo. At the very least, their verse has given voice to a new Muslim responsiveness to the United States' assertion of global legal sovereignty.

NOTES

1. Montasir al-Zayyat, *The Road to al-Qaeda: The Story of Bin Lāden's Right-Hand Man* (Sterling, Virginia: Pluto Press, 2004), p. 31.

2. Sayyid Qutb, *Muhammat al-Sha`ir fi al-Hayah wa Shi`r al-Jil al-Hadir* (Cairo: Dar al-Shuruq, 1933 [1974]), pp. 18–19.

3. Former Secretary of Defense Donald Rumsfeld has stated that the Guantánamo detainees are "among the most dangerous, best-trained, vicious killers on the face of the earth." The validity of such a claim is questioned by the Pentagon's own personnel at the base, some of whom have estimated that, at best, only a few dozen of the five hundred detainees have any connection with terrorism (Joseph Margulies, *Guantánamo and the Abuse of Presidential Power* (New York: Simon and Schuster, 2006), p. 211.

4. Susan Slyomovics, *The Performance of Human Rights in Morocco* (Philadelphia: University of Pennsylvania Press, 2005), pp. 10–11.

5. Ibid., pp. 191–92.

POEMS FROM GUANTÁNAMO

SHAKER ABDURRAHEEM AAMER

Shaker Abdurraheem Aamer is a Saudi Arabian citizen and British resident who has been detained at Guantánamo Bay since early 2002. The U.S. military alleges that he has ties to al Qaeda, apparently because of his work in Afghanistan for a Saudi charity—the Al-Haramain Foundation—suspected of funneling money to terrorist organizations. A leader among the Guantánamo detainees, Aamer helped broker an end to one of the hunger strikes. He elicited a concession from the military that it would allow the detainees to form a grievance committee and treat them in a manner consistent with the Geneva Conventions. In September, 2005, just days after the grievance committee was formed, the military disbanded it and sent Aamer to solitary confinement, where he remains today.

THEY FIGHT FOR PEACE

Peace, they say.
Peace of mind?
Peace on earth?
Peace of what kind?

I see them talking, arguing, fighting—
What kind of peace are they looking for?
Why do they kill? What are they planning?

Is it just talk? Why do they argue?
Is it so simple to kill? Is this their plan?

Yes, of course!
They talk, they argue, they kill—
They fight for peace.

ABDULAZIZ

Abdulaziz, who wishes not to reveal his last name, had just graduated from university in his native Riyadh, Saudi Arabia, when U.S. forces launched their attack on Afghanistan. He traveled to the region to find his brother and bring him home safely. Soon after Abdulaziz found him, both men were picked up by Northern Alliance forces. After being tortured in an Afghan prison, he was turned over to the U.S. military in early 2002 and eventually sent to Guantánamo along with his brother. Both were classified as enemy combatants. His brother was subsequently released, but Abdulaziz remains in detention.

O PRISON DARKNESS

O prison darkness, pitch your tent.
We love the darkness.

For after the dark hours of the night,
Pride's dawn will rise.

Let the world, with all its bliss, fade away—
So long as we find favor with God.

A boy may despair in the face of a problem,
But we know God has a design.

Even though the bands tighten and seem unbreakable,
They will shatter.

Those who persist will attain their goal;
Those who keep knocking shall gain entry.

O crisis, intensify!
The morning is about to break forth.

I SHALL NOT COMPLAIN

I shall not complain to anyone or expect grace from anyone
　　other than God, so help me God.

O Lord, my heart is plagued with troubles.

I shall not complain to anyone other than You, even if the seas
　　complain of dryness.

My spirit is free in the heavens, while my body is overpowered
　　by chains.

Praise God, who has granted me patience in times of adversity
　　and gratitude in times of gladness.

Praise God, who placed a garden and an orchard in my bosom,
　　so they will be with me always.

Praise God, who has granted me faith and made me a Muslim.

Praise God, Lord of the world.

ABDULLAH THANI FARIS AL ANAZI

Abdullah Thani Faris al Anazi is a double amputee,
having lost both of his legs in a U.S. bombing campaign
in Afghanistan while he was employed as a humanitarian
aid worker. After his first leg was amputated, he was arrested
on his recovery bed by bounty hunters and turned over to U.S.
forces. While in U.S. custody, his second leg was amputated.
He has been held at Guantánamo since 2002, where he has
received inadequate medical care. At times, he has been
forced to walk on prosthetic limbs held together with duct
tape.

TO MY FATHER

Two years have passed in far-away prisons,
Two years my eyes untouched by kohl.
Two years my heart sending out messages
To the homes where my family dwells,
Where lavender cotton sprouts
For grazing herds that leave well fed.

O Flaij, explain to those who visit our home
How I used to live.
I know your thoughts are swirled as in a whirlwind,
When you hear the voice of my anguished soul.
Send sweet peace and greetings to Bu'mair;
Kiss him on his forehead, for he is my father.
Fate has divided us, like the parting of a parent from a
    newborn.

O Father, this is a prison of injustice.
Its iniquity makes the mountains weep.
I have committed no crime and am guilty of no offense.
Curved claws have I,
But I have been sold like a fattened sheep.

I have no fellows but the Truth.
They told me to confess, but I am guiltless;
My deeds are all honorable and need no apology.
They tempted me to turn away from the lofty summit of
    integrity,
To exchange this cage for a pleasant life.
By God, if they were to bind my body in chains,
If all Arabs were to sell their faith, I would not sell mine.

I have composed these lines
For the day when your children have grown old.

O God—who governs creation with providence,
Who is one, singular and self-subsisting,
Who brings comfort and happy tidings,
Whom we worship—
Grant serenity to a heart that beats with oppression,
And release this prisoner from the tight bonds of
    ` confinement.

USTAD BADRUZZAMAN BADR

Ustad Badruzzaman Badr is a prolific Pakistani essayist
with an MA in English. Along with his brother Shaikh
Abdurraheem Muslim Dost, he spent much of the 1980s
publishing magazines that supported rebel fighters against
the Soviet occupation of Afghanistan and writing for the cause
of Pashtun nationalism. In November 2001 the brothers were
arrested by Pakistani intelligence officers, who subsequently
turned them over to the U.S. military. Badr was returned
to Peshawar in 2004 after the military determined that he
represented no threat to the United States. With his brother,
he recently published a memoir of his time in detention,
The Broken Shackles of Guantánamo.

LIONS IN THE CAGE

In the name of Allah, the Beneficent, the Most Merciful,
a poem written in Camp Delta, Guantánamo, Cuba

We are the heroes of the time.
We are the proud youth.
We are the hairy lions.

We live in the stories now.
We live in the epics.
We live in the public's heart.

We are the shield before the oppressor.
Our courage is like a mountain.
The Pharaoh of our time is restless because of us.

The Chief of the White Palace,
Like other sinful chiefs,
Cannot see our patience.

The whirlpool of our tears
Is moving fast towards him.
No one can endure the power of this flood.

It mostly happens, in these cages,
That the stars at midnight
Bring good news—

That we will surely succeed,
And the world will wait for us,
The Caravan of Badr.

MOAZZAM BEGG

Moazzam Begg is a British citizen who was arrested in Pakistan and detained for three years in Guantánamo. While there, Begg received a heavily-censored letter from his seven-year-old daughter; the only legible line was, "I love you, Dad." Upon his release, his daughter told him the censored lines were a poem she had copied for him: "One, two, three, four, five, / Once I caught a fish alive. / Six, seven, eight, nine, ten, / Then I let it go again." Released in 2005, he was never charged with a crime. The biggest problem at Guantánamo, he explained to Amnesty International, is "the sheer lack of any ability to prove your innocence because you remain in limbo, in legal limbo, and have no meaningful communication with your family." Begg recently published a memoir, *Enemy Combatant: My Imprisonment at Guantánamo, Bagram, and Kandahar.*

HOMEWARD BOUND

Begins this journey without reins,
Ends in capture without aims;
Now lying in the cell awake,
With merriment and smiles all fake:

Freedom is spent, time is up—
Tears have rent my sorrow's cup;
Home is cage, and cage is steel,
Thus manifest reality's unreal

Dreams are shattered, hopes are battered,
Yet with new status one is flattered!
The irony of it—detention, and all:
Be so small, and stand so tall.

Years of tears and days of toil
Are now but fears and tyrants' spoil;
Ordainment has surely come to pass,
But endure alone one must this farce.

Now "patience is of virtue" taught,
And virtue is of iron wrought;
So poetry is in motion set
(Perhaps, with appreciation met).

Still the paper do I pen,
Knowing what, but never when—
As dreams begin, and nightmares end—
I'm homeward bound to beloved tend.

JUMAH AL DOSSARI

Jumah al Dossari, a thirty-three-year-old Bahraini national, is the father of a young daughter. He has been held at Guantánamo Bay for more than five years. In addition to being detained without charge or trial, Dossari has been subjected to a range of physical and psychological abuses, some of which are detailed in *Inside the Wire*, an account of the Guantánamo prison by former military intelligence soldier Erik Saar. He has been held in solitary confinement since the end of 2003 and, according to the U.S. military, has tried to kill himself twelve times while in the prison. On one occasion, he was found by his lawyer, hanging by his neck and bleeding from a gash to his arm.

DEATH POEM

Take my blood.
Take my death shroud and
The remnants of my body.
Take photographs of my corpse at the grave, lonely.

Send them to the world,
To the judges and
To the people of conscience,
Send them to the principled men and the fair-minded.

And let them bear the guilty burden, before the world,
Of this innocent soul.
Let them bear the burden, before their children and before
    history,
Of this wasted, sinless soul,
Of this soul which has suffered at the hands of the "protectors
    of peace."

SHAIKH ABDURRAHEEM MUSLIM DOST

Shaikh Abdurraheem Muslim Dost is a Pakistani poet and essayist who spent nearly three years in Guantánamo with his brother, Ustad Badruzzaman Badr. Dost was a respected religious scholar, poet, and journalist—and author of nearly twenty books—before his arrest in 2001. While at Guantánamo, he composed thousands of lines of poetry in Pashto, most of which were retained by the U.S. military after his release in April 2005. In October 2006, shortly after Dost and his brother published a memoir of their Guantánamo detention, Dost was again arrested by Pakistani intelligence. He has not been heard from since.

THEY CANNOT HELP

In the name of Allah, the Beneficent, the Most Merciful,
a poem written in Camp Delta, Guantánamo, Cuba

Those who are charitable
Cannot help but sacrifice for others.

They cannot help but face danger
If they wish to remain true.

When they face injustice, dishonesty, and iniquity,
They cannot help but be under the power of the traitors and
    the notorious.

Consider what might compel a man
To kill himself, or another.

Does oppression not demand
Some reaction against the oppressor?

It is natural that a man is driven to invention
And to creation in times of duress.

The evildoer will be punished.
He cannot avoid making amends, and must apologize
    eventually.

Those who foolishly dispute with Dost the Poet
Cannot help but surrender, or else run away.

CUP POEM 1

What kind of spring is this,
Where there are no flowers and
The air is filled with a miserable smell?

CUP POEM 2

Handcuffs befit brave young men,
Bangles are for spinsters or pretty young ladies.

TWO FRAGMENTS

1.
Eid has come, but my father has not.
He is not come from Cuba.

I am eating the bread of Eid with my tears.
I have nothing.

Why am I deprived of the love of my father?
Why am I so oppressed?

2.
Just as the heart beats in the darkness of the body,
So I, despite this cage, continue to beat with life.

Those who have no courage or honor consider themselves free,
But they are slaves.

I am flying on the wings of thought,
And so, even in this cage, I know a greater freedom.

MOHAMMED EL GHARANI

Mohammed el Gharani, a fourteen-year-old Chadian
national raised in Saudi Arabia, had recently arrived in
Pakistan to learn English and to study information technology
when he was imprisoned by Pakistani police. They hanged
him by his wrists—nearly naked, his feet barely touching the
floor—and beat him if he moved. When told he would be
transferred to U.S. custody, Gharani was overjoyed, thinking
that his torture would end. Under U.S. custody in Kandahar,
Afghanistan, however, he was also stripped and beaten. In
January 2002, he became one of the first "enemy combatants"
transferred to Guantánamo Bay, where he remains. As many
as twenty-nine juveniles, including Gharani, have been
detained at Guantánamo in violation of international law.

FIRST POEM OF MY LIFE

Move it cautiously in the land of those who speak no Arabic,[1]
    Even if they gave you oaths bound by oaths.

Their aim is to worship petty cash,
    And for it they break all vows.

I came to their land to pursue an education,
    And saw such malice among them.

They surrounded the mosque, weapons drawn,
    As if they were in a field of war.

They said to us, "Come out peacefully,
    And don't utter a single word."

Into a transport truck they lifted us,
    And in shackles of injustice they bound us.

For sixteen hours we walked;
    For the entire time we remained in shackles.

All of us wanted to evacuate our bowels,
    But they insisted on denying us.

The soldier struck with his boot;
    He said we were all equally subjects.

In the prison's darkness they spread us out;
    In the cold's bitterness we sat.

When the red-faced infidels came to spend their money,
    Never had I seen such tribulation.

In a warplane they brought us up,
    And after a half hour, brought us down.

We saw such insults from them;
    Not even the book of God was protected.

Along with their malice, they were foolish.
    Tribulations, then hitting and imbecility.

For they are a people without reasonable minds,
    Due to their supply of alcoholic drinks.

The "Greasy"[2] arrived, in our state of need,
    On the condition that we raise the card with a cross.

"If you want dignity and protection,
    Then raise the cross for protection."

All of us threw the card away,
    Intent that our spirits be redeemed in sacrifice.

They carried us, afterwards, to Cuba,
    Because it is an afflicted isle.[3]

Out of spite, they showed such impudence.
    Their war is against Islam and justice.

translated by Flagg Miller

1. The author's first word, "Move it" (*emshi*), is couched in jarring colloquial Arabic. It is the kind of word used by non-Arabic speakers to give orders to prisoners. In initiating his verse with a vocabulary that flouts literary poetic standards, the poet suggests a kind of testimony that attempts to convey the starkness of his own experiences as a prisoner. My translation in the rest of the poem seeks to preserve the poet's bleak testimonial voice, conveyed in plain, often vernacular Arabic.

2. At the margin of his poem, the author explains that the word for "grease" (*salit*) is a pun on the word "cross" (*salib*), and specifies the International Red Cross, in particular. The word also plays upon the vernacular expression "His mind is greasy" (*'aqluh saliti*), suggesting that one's powers of reason are corrupted by sordid thoughts.

3. The poet's word for "afflicted" (*mankuba*) forms another pun with the word "Cuba" (*kuba*) in the previous line. Along with the previous line, the poet's choice of words evokes a discourse of resistance that has a Palestinian tenor. Redemption through sacrifice (*fida*) replicates the term used for Palestinian martyrs during the mid twentieth century (*fida'iyun*); acts of throwing (*rami*) suggest the stone-throwing tactics of the Palestinian Intifada, and the adjective "afflicted" evokes "The Affliction" (*al-Nakba*), the nickname given by Arabs to their 1948 defeat during Israel's war of independence. Note that such poetics immediately follow reference to the Red Cross, a symbol whose stirring associations for the author may be linked with early European Crusades in the region.

SAMI AL HAJ

Sami al Haj, a Sudanese national, was a journalist covering the conflict in Afghanistan for the television station al-Jazeera when, in 2001, he was taken into custody and stripped of his passport and press card. Handed over to U.S. forces in January 2002, he was tortured at both Bagram air base and Kandahar before being transferred to Guantánamo Bay in June 2002. The U.S. military alleges that he worked as a financial courier for Chechen rebels and that he assisted al Qaeda and extremist figures, but has offered the public no evidence in support of these allegations. Haj remains at Guantánamo.

HUMILIATED IN THE SHACKLES

When I heard pigeons cooing in the trees,
Hot tears covered my face.

When the lark chirped, my thoughts composed
A message for my son.

Mohammad, I am afflicted.
In my despair, I have no one but Allah for comfort.

The oppressors are playing with me,
As they move freely about the world.

They ask me to spy on my countrymen,
Claiming it would be a good deed.

They offer me money and land,
And freedom to go where I please.

Their temptations seize my attention
Like lightning in the sky.

But their gift is an evil snake,
Carrying hypocrisy in its mouth like venom.

They have monuments to liberty
And freedom of opinion, which is well and good.

But I explained to them that
Architecture is not justice.

America, you ride on the backs of orphans,
And terrorize them daily.

Bush, beware.
The world recognizes an arrogant liar.

To Allah I direct my grievance and my tears.
I am homesick and oppressed.

Mohammad, do not forget me.
Support the cause of your father, a God-fearing man.

I was humiliated in the shackles.
How can I now compose verses? How can I now write?

After the shackles and the nights and the suffering and the
    tears,
How can I write poetry?

My soul is like a roiling sea, stirred by anguish,
Violent with passion.

I am a captive, but the crimes are my captors'.
I am overwhelmed with apprehension.

Lord, unite me with my son Mohammad.
Lord, grant success to the righteous.

EMAD ABDULLAH HASSAN

Emad Abdullah Hassan is twenty-eight years old and from the port city of Aden, in Yemen. A prolific poet, he was taken into custody in Pakistan while studying at a university. He remains in Guantánamo, although the U.S. military does not allege that he has participated in any violence whatsoever.

THE TRUTH

Inscribe your letters in laurel trees,
From the cave all the way to the city of the chosen.

It was here that Destiny stood wondering.
Oh Night, are these lights that I see real?

* * *

I have observed the youths of Mohammed,
What splendid, righteous young men they are!

They have been scrubbed by events for years,
But that has only increased their keenness for the Lord.

They have been melted by events for years,
But that has only purified the gold from the dust.

Here, minds mature faster.
A day here is as two months at home.

* * *

Oh History, reflect. I will now
Disclose the secret of secrets.

My song will expose the damned oppression,
And bring the system to collapse.

The tyrants, full-equipped and numbered,
Stand unmoved in the face of the Light.

They proceed in the Dark, led by
The Devil, in pride and arrogance.

They have turned their land of peace
Into a home for hypocrites.

They have exchanged piety
For cheap commodity.

★ ★ ★

You, get up and question events.
Will you stand up to evil and oppression?

No, you will never settle for mere talk.
You believe the sword is the only arbiter.

★ ★ ★

Brothers, bear the weight of the heavy shackles,
Do not be confused by their wicked schemes.

Illusions soar all around this din,
Ropes are tied tightly to the wall,

And every evening, in lieu of a bride, they bring you
Distress and depression.

You have no companion but Night
To complain about bitter destiny.

You have no comrade but Night
To share in your sadness.

* * *

My Brother's yearning covers all the world,
His thoughts crowd the universe.

He sneaks away from slumber: Is anyone else awake?
No. His eyes tear without warning.

A noise rattles beneath his eyelids,
A hurricane echoes in his chest.

* * *

Behold, the face of the universe is dark,
As if its lights were covered by a curtain.

"Be patient and persevere!" These are Allah's words.
The fruit of patience is a running river.

For the sake of Allah, be patient and persevere.
Await God's promise to the righteous.

* * *

When the cloud departs from the East,
The face of the Earth cheers.

The sadness that suffocates him is lifted,
His thoughts turn to the Almighty.

He raises his hand to Heaven and cries,
"Oh God, you are the best of neighbors."

And when the Darkness threatens, he shouts,
"Away! Sleep not near me."

* * *

I am the Companion of the Night.

I am the one who refused humiliation in his own land,
Who found no repose.

I am the one who carried the burden on his neck,
Who refused to settle.

Oh Night, I am a bright light
That you will not obscure.

Oh Night, my song will restore the sweetness of Life:
The birds will again chirp in the trees,

The well of sadness will empty,
The spring of happiness will overflow,

And Islam will prevail in all corners of the Earth.
"Allahu Akbar, allahu Akbar." God is great.

They do not comprehend
That all we need is Allah, our comfort.

OSAMA ABU KABIR

Osama Abu Kabir is a Jordanian water truck driver who worked for the municipality of Greater Amman. After joining an Islamic missionary organization called Jama'at al-Tablighi, he traveled to Afghanistan, where he was detained by anti-Taliban forces and handed over to the U.S. military. One of the justifications offered for his continued detention is that he was captured wearing a Casio digital watch, a brand supposedly favored by members of al Qaeda because some models may be used as bomb detonators. Kabir remains at Guantánamo.

IS IT TRUE?

Is it true that the grass grows again after rain?
Is it true that the flowers will rise up in the Spring?
It is true that birds will migrate home again?
Is it true that the salmon swim back up their stream?

It is true. This is true. These are all miracles.
But is it true that one day we'll leave Guantánamo Bay?
Is it true that one day we'll go back to our homes?
I sail in my dreams, I am dreaming of home.

To be with my children, each one part of me;
To be with my wife and the ones that I love;
To be with my parents, my world's tenderest hearts.
I dream to be home, to be free from this cage.

But do you hear me, oh Judge, do you hear me at all?
We are innocent, here, we've committed no crime.
Set me free, set us free, if anywhere still
Justice and compassion remain in this world!

ADNAN FARHAN ABDUL LATIF

Adnan Farhan Abdul Latif is a twenty-seven-year old Yemeni from a family of modest means. The victim of a 1994 accident that resulted in serious head injuries, Latif spent much of the rest of the decade seeking affordable medical treatment in Jordan, Afghanistan, and Pakistan. Following the 9/11 attacks on the United States, he was taken into custody by Pakistani forces and turned over to the United States for a $5,000 bounty. He was eventually flown to Guantánamo and kept for a time in an open-air kennel exposed to the elements, causing further deterioration of his health. Latif has periodically joined other detainees in hunger strikes.

HUNGER STRIKE POEM

They are criminals, increasing their crimes.
They are criminals, claiming to be peace-loving.
They are criminals, torturing the hunger strikers.

They are artists of torture,
They are artists of pain and fatigue,
They are artists of insults and humiliation.

They are faithless—traitors and cowards—
They have surpassed devils with their criminal acts.

They do not respect the law,
They do not respect men,
They do not spare the elderly,
They do not spare the baby-toothed child.

They leave us in prison for years, uncharged,
Because we are Muslims.

Where is the world to save us from torture?
Where is the world to save us from the fire and sadness?
Where is the world to save the hunger strikers?

But we are content, on the side of justice and right,
Worshipping the Almighty.

And our motto on this island is, *salaam*.

OTHMAN ABDULRAHEEM MOHAMMAD

Othman Abdulraheem Mohammad is a twenty-six-year-old
Yemeni who, before being taken into custody by Pakistani
security forces at the Afghan border in late 2001, studied
law and taught the Qur'an in Afghanistan. While detained
by American forces in Kandahar, Mohammad witnessed
a Qur'an being thrown into a barrel of human waste. At
Guantánamo he has experienced a host of other affronts
to his religion, including the call to prayer being stopped
entirely. He has participated in camp-wide hunger strikes and
been subjected to force-feeding, in clear violation of both the
Geneva Conventions and World Medical Association protocols
for addressing prisoners who decline nourishment.

I AM SORRY, MY BROTHER

I am sorry, my brother.
The shackles bind my hands
And iron is circling the place where I sleep.

I am sorry, my brother,
That I cannot help the elderly or the widow or the little child.

Do not weigh the death of a man as a sign of defeat.
The only shame is in betraying your ideals
And failing to stand by your beliefs.

MARTIN MUBANGA

Martin Mubanga is a citizen of both the United Kingdom and Zambia. He was arrested in Zambia, where he and his sister were visiting relatives, and then transferred to Guantánamo without any legal process. While imprisoned there, Mubanga managed to inform his family about his mistreatment at Guantánamo by sending them letters, via the International Committee of the Red Cross, in the form of rap poetry. An athletic kickboxer, Mubanga was a frequent target of guard brutality. Released in early 2005, he lives in England, where he continues to campaign on behalf of the British residents who remain imprisoned at Guantánamo.

TERRORIST 2003

America sucks, America chills,
While d' blood of d' Muslims is forever getting spilled,
In d' streets of Nablus, in d' streets of Jenin,
Yeahhhhhhh! You know what I mean.

American gangstas, American lies,
In downtown LA, they was burning rubber tyres.
After Rodney King they woz burning 'nough fires.
Yeahhhhhhh! Them mother sumthing liars.

American justice, American pigs,
American soldiers, American wigs.
Yes I'm feeling angry, yes I'm feeling pissed,
An' it's about time that the JIF[1] got dissed.

Now them ask me, what will ya do if ya leave the prison?
Will ya be able to slip back into d' system?
What ya gonna do with ya new-found fame?
An' will ya ever, ever go *jihad* again?

An' them er says to me, if ya's walking down d' street,
Sees a fine girl will ya sweep her off her feet?
Or leave her standing thinking that she sweet,
For the next mans to come and reap?

An' them er says to me, now you's back from d' core,
You're a terrorist, a big-time hardcore.
But my friends them know the score,
Cause back in d' day me use to g'waan juss like a whore.
Now me a Muslim, so me whan f' shut that door.

But the government's them, them a feeling sore!
Cause like a page in a book you know me done a tore
A hole in them heart, them exposing hypocrisy,
For all the world them to clearly come 'n see.

Now them ask me, will ya come work for us?
Had to hold my breath so they would not hear me cuss,
Dumb mother sumthings, I'd rather suck pus,
Than work for the mans that Allah did a cuss.

An' them a says to me, we can make your life sweet,
Give you all the things you ever wanted to eat.
All you got to do is practice deceit,
An' everything a go be really neat.

"*Sauf ofaker fi haza.* Let me think about it."
Qurrratu Qur'an.[2] There was no need to doubt it,
Did you think for a second I really did doubt it?
There wasn't even need for me to go shout it.

They're scum, they're criminals, on their way to hell,
And not for all of the *dunya*[3] would I join them as well!

Now me's coming with these lyrics from Guantánamo B,
In my prison cell down by the sea,
For hard-core detainees like you an' me,
Terrorist 2003,
So called. Yeah, that's me!

NOTES

1. Acronym for Joint Interrogation Facility at Guantánamo.

2. Arabic for "I read the Qur'an."

3. Arabic for worldly, material things as opposed to spiritual matters.

ABDULLA MAJID AL NOAIMI,
THE CAPTIVE OF DIGNITY

Abdulla Majid al Noaimi is a twenty-four-year-old citizen of
Bahrain who attended Old Dominion University in Virginia,
but returned home after a year, heartbroken over breaking
up with his girlfriend. Shortly after beginning his electrical
engineering studies in the United Arab Emirates in 2001,
Noaimi traveled to Afghanistan to find a family member who
had not been heard from in some time. After an unsuccessful
search, he made his way to the Pakistani border and asked
to be taken to the Bahrain embassy. Instead, Pakistani
authorities turned him over to the U.S. military. He was
detained in Kandahar, Afghanistan, for about five months
before being transferred to Guantánamo. He was released
from the prison camp in November 2005.

I WRITE MY HIDDEN LONGING

I write my hidden longing:

I tried to defend him with my eyes,
But I looked around and was cornered.
Destiny had found me.

My rib is broken,
And I can find no one to heal me.

My body is frail,
And I can see no relief ahead.

Before me is a tumultuous sea;
The land continues to call me.
But I am sailing in my thoughts.

The impious have murdered me in my home.

I wish someone would comfort me;
At night I taste bile and cannot sleep.

The tears of someone else's longing are affecting me;
My chest cannot take the vastness of emotion.

The book of God consoles me,
And dulls the pains I have suffered.
The book of God assuages my misery,
Even though they declared war against it.

I stand tall and smile in the face of misery.
I am satisfied.

Oh Father, tell the tearful one,
"Do not forget me, as I do not forget you."
He will understand my condition.

And when you pass by life's familiar objects—
The Bedouin rugs, the bound branches,
The flight of pigeons—
Remember me.

I salute the brothers,
And pray peace to those who remain faithful.
I say hello to Shwayman,
And to everyone whom I love,
And to every one who misses me.

Remember, pray to God for those whom I love.
Maybe God, with His kindness, will have mercy on me.

MY HEART WAS WOUNDED BY THE STRANGENESS

This is a poem that I have written about my brother and friend Salman al Khalifa at the Guantánamo prison, after a long separation between us. The Americans were keen on keeping us apart. Four months later, he sent verbal greetings with the brothers, in which he said, "May Peace, God's Mercy and Blessings be upon you. I miss you a great deal and I'm trying to write a poem for you." I felt guilty about this. Will he write a poem for me when he is no poet, while I, who claim to be a poet, have written nothing for him?

I then said, "If he writes a poem for me before I write one for him, I deserve to be scoffed at until the Day of Judgment." So I set out to write, but I could not concentrate on the poem. I put poetry writing aside and turned to memorizing the Qur'an. But then I could not concentrate on the Qur'an, because my mind was occupied with the poem. With my mind divided, time began to pass. And then I was inspired:

My heart was wounded by the strangeness.
Now poetry has rolled up his sleeves, showing a long arm.

Time passes. The hands of the clock deceive us.
Time is precious and the minutes are limited.

Do not blame the poet who comes to your land,
Inspired, arranging rhymes.

Oh brother, who need not be named, I send you
My gift of greetings. I send heavily falling rains

To quench your thirst and show my gratitude.
My poem will comfort you and ease your burdens.

If you blame yourself, my poem will appease you.
My mind is not heavy with animosity.

I will be satisfied once you are free, and I will embrace you.
There is nothing, brother, like a mild, agreeable temper.

I will offer advice out of pure cordiality—
Advice from one who has experienced the impossible:

You will not gain everything that your soul desires;
Some things will come to you, but others will not.

Forget what people say and be satisfied with who you are.
Patience, the bony animal, will lead you to meat.

Be generous to others, brother,
And leave behind your avaricious spirit.

If your brother has hurt you,
Recall his good deeds and the pain will go away.

Hide the sadness of your heart as in a valley.
Make it your captive; if released, it will make you suffer.

No matter how long our separation lasts, I will not forget you.
What is hidden in our hearts is expressed in my words.

You are precious and grow more precious.
He who has companions like you will never lose dignity.

I hope that your nights will always be cheerful.
May the Lord compensate you for what you have lost.

I ask the Merciful One to guide you to peace.
May the Lord keep you fast on the path of virtue.

I conclude my poem by invoking prayers and blessings,
On the messenger of Allah, Ahmed, his chosen one.

IBRAHIM AL RUBAISH

Ibrahim al Rubaish was teaching in Pakistan when he was arrested by mercenaries and sold to allied forces. A religious scholar who dislikes hostility and was once a candidate for a judgeship, Rubaish has a daughter, born just three months before he was captured, who is now five years old. During a military administrative hearing, he was told, "If you are considered to be a continued threat, you will be detained. If you are not considered a threat, we will recommend release. Why should we consider releasing you?" Rubaish's response was, "In the world of international courts, the person is innocent until proven guilty. Why, here, is the person guilty until proven innocent?"

ODE TO THE SEA

O Sea, give me news of my loved ones.

Were it not for the chains of the faithless, I would have dived
    into you,
And reached my beloved family, or perished in your arms.

Your beaches are sadness, captivity, pain, and injustice.
Your bitterness eats away at my patience.

Your calm is like death, your sweeping waves are strange.
The silence that rises up from you holds treachery in its fold.

Your stillness will kill the captain if it persists,
And the navigator will drown in your waves.

Gentle, deaf, mute, ignoring, angrily storming,
You carry graves.

If the wind enrages you, your injustice is obvious.
If the wind silences you, there is just the ebb and flow.

O Sea, do our chains offend you?
It is only under compulsion that we daily come and go.

Do you know our sins?
Do you understand we were cast into this gloom?

O Sea, you taunt us in our captivity.
You have colluded with our enemies and you cruelly guard us.

Don't the rocks tell you of the crimes committed in their
   midst?
Doesn't Cuba, the vanquished, translate its stories for you?

You have been beside us for three years, and what have you
   gained?
Boats of poetry on the sea; a buried flame in a burning heart.

The poet's words are the font of our power;
His verse is the salve for our pained hearts.

SIDDIQ TURKESTANI

Siddiq Turkestani is a thirty-three-year-old ethnic Uighur raised in Saudi Arabia. In 1997, while traveling in Afghanistan, he was abducted by members of al Qaeda and tortured until he "confessed" to plotting to kill Osama bin Laden. He was imprisoned by the Taliban at Kandahar until 2001, when U.S. intelligence personnel visited the jail. He told them his story and was promised a quick release. Instead, he was eventually sent to Guantánamo and held for four years on accusations that included being associated with the Taliban and al Qaeda. The military determined that he was not an enemy combatant in January 2005 and he was released from Guantánamo nearly six months later.

EVEN IF THE PAIN

Even if the pain of the wound increases,
There must be a remedy to treat it.

Even if the days in prison endure,
There must be a day when we will get out.

WHERE THE BURIED FLAME BURNS

ARIEL DORFMAN

Three decades ago, when I was living in exile and my country, Chile, was being devastated by a dictatorship, I met a woman who had been arrested by agents of Pinochet's secret police and then tortured endlessly in a cellar in Santiago.

It was poetry, she told me that day in Paris, which had allowed her to survive. In the fierce darkness of her ordeal, she repeated to herself those verses sent from some dead poet, she said, as a way of differentiating herself from the men who were treating her body like an object, like a piece of meat. That was how she protected her besieged identity, the one thing those jailers could not touch, could not deny her, could not erase: just some words, just some precarious, almost evanescent, words from the past as a defense against what seemed an eternity of pain and humiliation.

It is shameful and yet also wondrous that I immediately evoked that woman as soon as I began to read the poems from the prisoners at Guantánamo.

Shameful because it is the United States, supposedly a democracy, that is treating its detainees in the same brutal manner that dictatorial Chile and countless other desolate governments across the planet have treated their own captives. Shameful because it is the United States, supposedly a beacon of freedom, that has tortured these "enemy combatants" and denied them the basic human rights all men and women on our earth possess, regardless of whatever crimes they may or may not have committed. Shameful because it is the United States, supposedly a model of justice to be globally envied and imitated, that has locked up these men indefinitely, refused to charge them or put them on trial, blocked them from communicating with their families and the outside world, degraded their humanity, and abused their religion and convictions to pressure them into "confessing" their "terrorist links."

And wondrous, yes. The fact that men held in the most appalling, the most desperate conditions, recur like that woman from Chile did, to poetry as a response to the violence they are subjected to, can anything give us more hope for our species?

These prisoners, let us remember, could not be sure, when their minds groped for words to sing their sad nights, that anyone other than their God would listen or would care. They did not intend these poems for publication; indeed, had probably no expectation that their isolated verses would even reach their fellow prisoners, let alone the wider world. Some of the words they composed are haunted with beauty. Others are less accomplished. There are those who are almost fanatically militant and those who only crave the serenity of home, the absent mother, father, son. A few considered themselves poets before they were captured, while most appear to have discovered the power of sounds and syllables once they found themselves, for the first time, cut off from the life and family and landscape they had always known. Some trust in God and some trust the dawn and some have no trust left at all. But every one of them seems to have understood that to express his anguish in writing was a wager against despair, a way of affirming his defiant humanity.

In this, they were encouraged, certainly, by their Muslim religion, which believes that the Written Word is sacred and that the curves and flow of the Script in which their Prophet's sayings were transcribed are mirrors of the divine. And the Guantánamo detainees were undoubtedly assisted as well by a tradition, prevalent in the cultural environment where they originally grew up, proclaiming reverence for poets.

And yet, something else, I suspect, is going on, something which joins them to that woman tortured in Chile and to so many other victims in so many relentless dungeons elsewhere who have, since the beginning of history, as a response to the worst abandonment, also used poetry to redeem their wounded dignity.

What I sense is that the ultimate source of these poems from Guantánamo is the simple, almost primeval, arithmetic of breathing in and breathing out.

The origin of life and the origin of language and the origin of poetry are all there, in each first breath, each breath as if it were our first, the anima, the spirit, what we inspire, what we expire, what separates us from extinction, minute after minute, what keeps us alive as we inhale and exhale the universe.

And the written word is nothing more than the attempt to make that breath permanent and secure, carve it into rock or mark it on paper or sign it on a screen, so that its cadence will endure beyond us, outlast our breath, break the shackles of solitude, transcend our transitory body and touch someone with its waters.

Breathing in and breathing out.

What these prisoners shared with their jailers, what they shared with the men who incarcerated them and feared them and saw them only as the enemy.

Poetry as a call to those who breathe the same air to also breathe the same verses, to bridge the gap between bodies and between cultures and between warring parties.

And that is the deeper, and perhaps more paradoxical, significance of the appearance of these poems in the United States, rescued by American lawyers, printed by an American press, copyedited by American eyes, published in the very heartland, the very center, of the nation that has so maltreated these men.

Think of the prisoners, breathing in and breathing out those words, close by an ocean they can hear nearby but never see and never touch. Think of them, now represented to their faraway foes by words of fire and sorrow, asking us to listen, to acknowledge the buried flame of their existence. Think that we have a chance to help them complete the journey that started in a cage inside a concentration camp, merely by something as simple as reading these poems. Think that perhaps someday, perhaps soon, if we care enough, if we are troubled enough, it will not be just the verses that are set free to roam the world but the hands and lips and lungs that composed them.

Until that day arrives, their true home, rather than the infamous detention center at Guantánamo Bay, will be the bitter poems they have written against loneliness and death.